A TUG OF BLUE

First published in 2016 by
The Dedalus Press
13 Moyclare Road
Baldoyle
Dublin D13 K1C2
Ireland

www.**dedaluspress**.com

ISBN 978 1 910251 22 5

Dedalus Press titles are represented in the UK by
Central Books, 99 Wallis Road, London E9 5LN
and in North America by Syracuse University Press, Inc.,
621 Skytop Road, Suite 110, Syracuse, New York 13244

Cover painting: 'Fair Enough' by Alicia Armstrong
By kind permission of the artist
http://aliciaannearmstrong.com

The Dedalus Press receives financial assistance from
The Arts Council / An Chomhairle Ealaíon.

A TUG OF BLUE

Eleanor Hooker

DEDALUS PRESS

ACKNOWLEDGEMENTS

My thanks to the editors of the following journals and periodicals where these poems, or earlier versions, were first published: *Poetry* (Chicago), *PN Review* (UK), *Poetry Ireland Review, The Stinging Fly, The Moth, POEM: International English Language Quarterly* (UK), *Cyphers, The Irish Times, The Irish Examiner, Southword, New Dublin Press, The Ofi Press* (Mexico), *The Pickled Body, artPAPIER* (in translation, Poland), *The Enchanting Verses* (India), *Blackjack* (in translation, Dublin/Romania), *Banshee and Skylight 47.*

'A Rite' was awarded 1st Prize 2013 Trocaire/Poetry Ireland Poetry Competition, 'Irrepressibly Bare' was long-listed 2014 Fish Poetry Prize and nominated for a Pushcart Prize by the Ofi Press, 'A Calling' was Highly Commended in the 2016 Gregory O'Donoghue International Poetry Prize, 'Weathering' was shortlisted for the Troubadour Poetry Prize 2013. Other poems have been broadcast on RTÉ Radio 1 and Prosody, a National Public Radio, Pittsburgh, USA, also Literature Out Loud, Robert Morris University's Literary Radio Show, Pittsburgh, USA. 'Conceive' was requested by UK poet Rebecca Goss for her blog on Heart Poems for Children's Heart Week 2014. 'Watermarked' was commissioned by Patricia McCarthy, Editor at Agenda, for the Winter 2013 issue commemorating Seamus Heaney

Warm thanks to all those who provided encouragement, comments and their time as first readers of these poems, but especially James Harpur, Thomas McCarthy and John Glenday. My grateful thanks to Tess Barry, Jan Beatty and Clodagh Beresford Dunne for their belief in poems that might otherwise have become strays. My sincere thanks to Pat Boran at Dedalus Press, for his keen editorial eye.

Huge thanks to Alicia Armstrong for the use of her fabulous image 'Fair Enough' as the cover image of my book.

CONTENTS

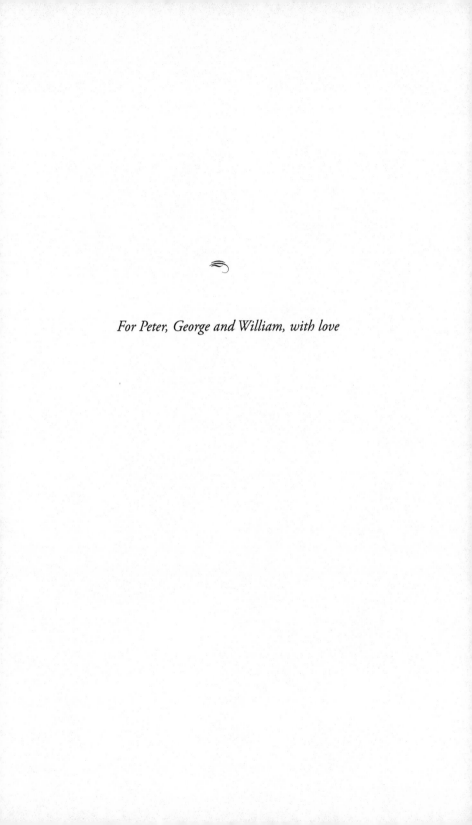

For Peter, George and William, with love

I

If I were asked to construct
a world that wasn't there

I'd make every surface
scrupulously blue, and you
the only resident.

from *Blue* by John Glenday

Weathering

I keep my appointment with Rain.
We meet in the wrong room. Upstairs.
Rain is … melancholy. She rinses
a naked bulb that hung itself
on white wire. *It ran out of light*,
she says, spreading her fall
from the room's unfathomed sky.

Rain enquires if I've brought questions.
I am allowed four. Four only.
Before I can deny it, she presses
her sodden lips to mine.
Not now, she says. *They are come.*

The sash windows unlace their gowns
so that ghost ships, dragging nets
filled with memories absolved
by Rain, can sail through them.

And as we watch, Rain says,
These are your questions:
Why is it they hide in there?
Why is it they turn from me?
Is it to the same place they go?
And is it the same story they weather?

Rain says, *there is no tenderness*
in the absence of joy, and, in the absence
of joy, songbirds squabble.

When there is nothing left to say,
Rain envelops me; her hair lies on my face
like tears, and inside my closed mouth,
hummingbirds fly backwards into my throat.

Upended

And afraid.

Everything gets through.
Rain pushes under slates
and spits on the floor.

Wind moans in the walls
as darkness shuffles through
rooms, jarring the shade.

I am a solitary creature who
is told not to be a solitary
creature, to let others in.

Into what, I wonder,
there's just me and an echo
in here; an echo that cries
over and over,

Let me out
Let me out

Escape Route

You fix our ladder in the scorched earth,
watch as the crows crowd round us.
I hear their cautionary caw-caws and cover
your ears against their thin black sermons.

And so we climb. Me. Then you.

Runged, we stroke each bird,
'sedate and clerical' –
one bestows a molted quill feather,
colour-run like oil-marked silk.

Is it an omen? You ask. *Should we go back?*
I don't answer; I'm too busy holding up the sky.

'Sedate and clerical' is how Charles Dickens described
the crow in *The Mystery of Edwin Drood*

To Stay Going

Rain fell like a punishment there.
It lashed his stooped back
when he footed turf, while ravens,
black as guilt, jabbered at him.

They say he was cursed from the day
he stole those raven's eggs. Say it's why
the lake hid his blue-eyed girl. Some say
ravens became his friends, say they carried the colour
of his lost littlin in their eyes. Others deny it; say it's only
    a *piseog*;
say 'tis known those birds neither forget nor forgive.

His dog was his shadow.
Said it crawled out of the lake as a pup. They say he buried
that dog after it's eyes turned, say he near went mad,
say he told them those eyes were of his missing bairn.

Truth is, he rarely spoke, and only when he'd something
to say. And O I listened, he being the only man worth
hearing ever I'd known. When a harvest moon lit corridors
through the woods, we walked them through. In there
he spoke the secret world of words. He drew me a map,
so I would know a path in, have a way out.

He was my friend.
He told me to go and stay going, said 'twould be a death
if I came back. Made me smell his hair, face, hands,
worn geansey, said if once I longed for peat-smoke
in my nostrils, yearned for home in a turf fire,
to recollect that smell, and it's shame, and how
it left a stain of poverty on his person.

They say ravens ringed the chimney crown with blackthorn sticks, say they caught and set the thatch. Others say difference makes stupid men afraid, enough to douse bulrushes and touch the roof while he slept.

A Weather Eye

The afternoon a dead calf drifted to our shore
was not the first unexpected happening of the day.
The calf, bloated under vellum, her brown boots
fastened by reeds, lay with her head extended
and right eye fixed on an empty sky. Fearful.
But water is tender to the dead, and will return
what it cannot own … eventually.

I make two calls. I tell them of the calf.
They say, *you okay?*
They say, *check its tag.*
They say, *wait.*
They say, *do nothing else 'till we're there.*

I step into the shallows, and water, sensing access,
attempts to fill my boots. As I crouch, the dead calf
lifts her head, drunkenly. She fixes on my dogs,
but they are good creatures; they sit and wait
when told. She turns her frozen gaze to mine,
tilts her head that I may see the pink serrated
edge of bone, where ear and tag
are severed. She senses the buzzards
I know are watching from their loop of sky.

Some days, exhausted by the sights daylight
thrusts upon us, we collapse early into the
bony hours of dark. The afternoon a dead
calf came to our shore was one such day,
with nothing to be done by us 'till sunrise,
and at sunrise she was gone. Wind had
changed, so water took her elsewhere.

Doppelgänger

after Neruda

When did she come in search of me? I cannot say.
Out of the lake and into the air, forever
marked by dusk, she is nourished by under-earth
fusty decay. Blue in summer, green eyed in winter,
I don't believe she has screeched in any of our collaborations.
Yet it's others she favours with ancient eucalyptus,
with willow myrtles. I am her pupil too,
and would love her more than she needs me to hate her.
In deadly night she gives me *Atropa Belladonna*,
dilates my pupils so wide that the light in everything
is expressed and swallowed and expressed.
She hums Prokofiev, while I try to discover
the words for her song in my own slurred voice.

Mirrored

She visited again last night, no pike this time.
She was singing too, her song the sound of a heavy body
dragging itself, deadly, up the stairs. Her malady
not too dissimilar to that thud-thump heartbeat
in my ears. She brought mirrors into my mind
and in my mind she filled the mirrors with crows,
huge-beaked, hungry crows. That fed. And though
I couldn't move, I kept my eyes open,
I wasn't frightened; I knew sooner or later I'd wake,
and she would have to take her mirrors and her crows,
leaving my pulse behind.

Nailing Wings to the Dead

Since we nail
wings to the dead,
she calls ravens
from the sky
to inspect our work. "For flight,"
they say, "first remove their boots."

She leans in,
inspects a fresh hex
behind my eyes,
takes my feet
and lays them on the fire,
to burn it out, roots first.

We're the last,
Babička and me.
We've survived on
chance and bread
baked from the last store of grain.
And as we're out of both,

we will die soon.
They are gathering
in the well.
We disrobe.
She hums whilst I nail her wings,
she tells me a tale, her last gift –

"This dark stain,
passed kiss to kiss-stained
fevered mouth,
blights love, is pulsed
by death-watch beetle's
tick, timing our decay.

They know this.
They wait by water,
gulping despair.
The ravens keep watch,
they say the contagion's here,
they promise to take us first."

Her tale done,
we go wingèd and naked
to the well.
We hear them
climbing the walls, caterwauling.
But ravens are swift, and swoop.

Guardian Angel

after Guy Denning

Mine is perpetually undressed, though
not ingloriously so. He's illustrated too,

yet I can tell his new tattoo,
Paradis Est Ici, does not improve his spirits.

When he splays his charcoaled wings,
the wrench of skin, feather and bone

makes a sound like splintering wood,
I hear him mutter, "fuck, that hurts".

He shaved his head when I shaved
mine aged twenty-two, and though

my hair's grown back, still he calls me
'baldylocks'. I've been called worse.

With a devoted sense of wickedness
he feeds rosemary to lambs: "Pre-seasoning,"

he winks, "no salvation for the lamb".
He's at his most morose in a boat;

it reminds him of biblical times and
fishing trips that brought him little cheer.

He gets cantankerous at my dithering,
tells me I need a "swift kick up the arse".

"You *must* rid yourself of your demons,"
he chides. "What," I snap, "and lose you?"

Lucid Dreaming

I need to go back, stay there for long
enough to speak to my feathered Shaman;
I need to tell him I was wrong
to be mad with the waterman,
his howling at the sea's swell.
I check my watch, look away then back
and nine hours have passed; a dream's *tell*.
In this lucid otherworld the only lack
is colour, the exceptions being my Shaman's
canker eyes, his blond shriveled wings. My plan
is to find him, remind him how as my dæmon
he must take the sea's chill from my bones, that began
with the drownings, let me sing truth
to the dark and forgive me the fault-lines of my youth.

Anatomy of Deceit

A riddle,
it plays soundless games,
soundlessly.
Its crow's feet
tap at nursery doors, its coarse
knock, a nightmare's lullaby.

It is hush
in the conch shell that
is not the sea,
but which compels
you to press it closer
to your ear, that it may enter.

It is the eel
that eats the eyes
of the drowned,
and being
the temperature
of loss, it is ravenous.

It will climb
the water lily,
suck silence
from its heart.
It is spin, a noxious spew
from Shelob's spinneret.

It tells you
it loves you, its love
is the taste
of blue-clotted milk,
sand-suckled blue.
Its love starves every hunger.

A Latterday Aithirné

Without judgment, we took him in, our guest,
in accordance with the laws of hospitality,
did so with kindliness. Others will attest
to this. Our care, which in reality
is given all of visiting bards,
was to feed him at our table, to give
lodging for his stay, to discard
misgivings at the costive
nature of his gift. Another instance
does exist, when Aithirné the Importunate
took the seeing eye in tribal vengeance.
That we live in gentler times is fortunate
for us, no bloodied lake shall come of this.
So he may spin his guerdon, his thankless hiss.

So spin your guerdon, your thankless hiss.
For us no bloodied lake shall come of this.
That we live in gentler times is fortunate,
so take the seeing eye in tribal vengeance,
we insist. Like Aithirné the Importunate,
you abuse our gift to feign an instance
of revulsion, and in that savage
lodgment that you made, you disregard
us that fed you at our table, that gave
you all was given any visiting bard –
our care, which in reality
we gave with kindliness, as history will attest.
Indifferent to the laws of hospitality,
and full of judgment, you took us in, our guest.

Janus

I dared not look at the back
of her head, through her
long black hair, to where
she hid her other face.

The hair on her arms
wafted like dark sea
grass, which, when she
molted, fell like charged pins.

You said her black hairy
tongue was a condition.
I think it was the lies
she told, secrets she hid.

Once, I saw her pluck
hairs from her groin.
Each bulbous root
swollen with a foetus,

which she threw away.
*That's where babies
come from*, she said,
as her other face cried.

Not at Any Cost

She followed me. I let her.
Her mask slipped.
I saw her drive. She let me.
Nobody will believe you, she said.
She unlatched her bolt-top
head, exposed two rows
of concentric teeth crunching
fresh quarry, cracking bones.
I declined to be taught
her ways. She let me go.

Rules of the Game

The first rule is, there are no rules
that distinguish you. You must know that
before you allow yourself to be the fool –
a lone player in this artificial spat.

You must know that
your opponent may well be yourself,
a lone player in this artificial spat,
battling the formidable opposition of self.

Yes, your opponent may well be yourself,
puzzling rules applied to a single player re-creation,
battling the formidable opposition of self
in a game of charades. Resist the temptation

to puzzle rules applied to a single player recreation.
And before you play the fool
in a game of charades, resist the temptation.
The first rule is, there are no rules.

Insight

i.m. Michael Hartnett

And just because the stand of oaks was blind
she gave them eyes; iridescent glow stones
from fathomless seas. And once inclined
to hold the sky with seasoned hands grown
out of touch, they cupped the light, dappled
it for shadows and for shade. Now in sight
of things they know the shape of, they grapple
with her lonely walks on moonless nights.
They whisper to each other, *even the sky is alone tonight.*
She presses her eyes to their eyes and inside their world
she finds you there, naked surgeon, a light
by your well, your body unfurled
as the stars flow through you, to trace
your hopeful song, so *music is heard in space.*

The Present

I went inside a clock. My dæmon
unlocked the back, told me to take
my time as he laced me into my snow
boots. Nervous, I almost forgot the present.

In the Blizzard Room, snow globes
bloomed on icicle-spears. A Mammoth
nudged a blown orb along a frozen gully.
Preserved inside the glass was my old schoolroom.
Chalk flakes dusted the gaping floorboards,
and huddled beneath the timbers
were my classmates, silent and petrified.

My dæmon took me by the hand
and led me to the Room of Rankings;
a parched, outside-inside plot. Ladders,
fixed in caked earth, leaned against
a bruising sky. My dæmon said, *a bruising sky
has dealt beatings, it can no longer assure the stars,
let us go from here.* So we left it to its shame.

In the Lens Room, the clock face turned
to follow us. At the centre of the chamber
I hummed my tuneless rhyme, and from one wall
my little girl stepped out of time, she clutched
my tattered present. *You mustn't hold on, let her go now,
let her be,* my dæmon said as I drew her close.

Irrepressibly Bare

It is not thunder. It is her Grandpa's old oak desk,
dragging itself about in the attic, searching for a slip
of slate that lets in the sky. While the basilisk
sleeps, she will risk a further ascent into the dark, trip
up and up the soundless stair to renew her scholarship
in rain, in separations. Once she tempts the desk with diabetic ink
drops, it will allow her access to the Affairs of Hail, to a Fellowship
in The Departed. An attic chest coughs camphor musk, a lurid stink
that preserves the unused baptismal gown, but rusts her doll's slow
    blink,
makes it cry black tears. The desk unbolts, coaxes her back
with an archangel of nightingales, with song letters unburned; links
to the green man who delivered her world, her periodic insomniac.
But *the past is a foreign country: they do things differently there*,
there can be no return, consequence must be borne, irrepressibly
    bare.

A Calling

I kneel where the water frays, and from my hands
build the cracked prayer of a cup.
— John Glenday

The night is a drowned woman
in off the lake to waken me.
She is filled with stones and moulded
by the weight of fog. She sings me
from the nightmare that you have died
in a foreign land. I hear you calling.

Anchored offshore is the great hull
of *Humanity*, waiting for the dark
to lessen, for the fog to lift.
I launch my boat over a crunch
of stones and, jumping in, snag on
traces of the dead taking shape.

Each pull on the oars is a rhythm
of curl, splash, settle and silence,
and that last I fear more than
the Siren's song. Solitary boats
rise out of the fog and when I try
to call, *Have you seen my son?*

the sound from my throat is a gull's
screech and then they are gone once more.
Humanity looms, unrigged and waiting
for the black caw from the crow
manacled to its nest. And there, I see you
atop the mizzenmast, sheltered by
the canvas-sail wings of seabirds.

You are smiling the smile you braved
as a small boy in a yard of bullies,
but I am reassured by your point
of safety, your access to flight.
I do not call out through the thinning silence,

I row coordinates of a reciprocal journey
to the ragged edge of sleep. In three days you
will call to tell me of your dream; of me rowing
through fog, silently mouthing your name.

Storm Song

The autumn line-storm bears the lake
to my door, and in the pounding water
is my menagerie of three-eyed fish, and
in the ardent air – an arabesque of ravens and rooks.

This porous house has never resisted,
the wind unknots and they all rain in.
Once inside, my fishes and the birds
resume their routine of swim and storm song.

I find breathing space on a bloated chest,
rise to the rafters with a raven and a rook
beside me, monitoring the flood. Attic curtains
spinnaker, and the house runs before the wind.

In large dense shoals, my fish dive free
to the deepest available water, drawing
down the broken echoes of my humming,
sending back up the stormy shadows of my song.

Ablution

Ghost me. Fossil me.
Resurrect me near dawn.
— *Traci Brimhall*

On my father's side
I am part fish.
When I am dead,
return me to water.

That part of me
which is raven, on
my mother's side,
will submit.

Do not waste time.
Do not bury me,
or feed me to maggots.
Return me to water,

I've shown you where.
The flow is steady
at this Point.
Don't reduce me to ash.

Petrify me.
Bed me in the fresh lake
whose virtue is
to harden heart to stone.

The sediment
will own me, preserve me
from foragers,
minerals will fill me,

form stone-crystal
casts of every sealed cell,
death-bound inside me.
Return me to water

and no church please,
this is my wish.
From my father's side
I am part fish.

Silence

Non chiudere le mie labbra aprendo le tue
— *Umberto Eco*

Hoarse from speaking to herself
she seals her lips with a single suture.

She has trapped her voice inside, screams
no longer cut her lips to draw another's blood.

She believes she will sail deeper oceans on this avowal
of silence. She becomes weightless swallowing

words her thoughts prompt her not to speak.
When I unpick the stitch, she mumbles she has no desire

to be saved. As she steps up to the liferaft, I take
her hand, alarmed by this new storm blowing through us.

Encrypted

They put us in the crypt,
my twin and I. She died
before we were born –
oh many years ago.
I eat the dark so she can see me.
She plucks an acorn from my iris,
says my eyes are the precise colour
of forest floor she'd imagined.
Tugging at my raven-wings,
she asks to keepsake one black feather.
She swims in my sea-skirt
and, when she tires,
gathers perfect pebbles.
A collector, I think.
I've resolved to collect you too,
she murmurs, counting six
fingers on her left hand.

Love Song

for Peter

Remember when I came to you
clothed only in catastrophe?
You whispered, "If I unbolt my heart,
you must walk through or walk away."
Remember? And once inside, we coupled,
unlearned the sad refrain we once called loneliness.
We became the boat. Reefed our sails
in squally weather, sailed our course together.
When judgment fell
and the fleet railed "recollect your family's
good name, *we're* your class remember",
you gave my tears to the sea and the sea
wept. They hauled our sheet
through the block, and when our boat luffed,
we corrected, we stemmed the line.
And after the wind arrived as a huge silence,
I asked if we could ever be becalmed
and you said no, we *have locked
ourselves inside one heart,* remember.

Skipping Stones

A rare day and the lake is a tug of blue
and the haul of water is a tow of sky,
and I stop in my quiet place
to skip stones, mindful of change.
She doesn't pass by, she stops to say
they're having a bash to which
everyone we know is going and,
well, since it's up to her ...

I retreat to my quiet place,
mindful of change, aware that
the multiple bounce of stones is
dependent on the angle at which
they're thrown, and the object
is to skip as many times
as possible, before sinking.

The Sheltered World

We navigate the narrow neck
of darkness to find them in the gut
of the night – fouled, stricken, wrecked.
We return them to the sheltered world,

and in returning to the sheltered world
we sup at the Still, our land-legs hollow
but restless to put to sea restored.
Cradling a carafe of light, an ancient seafarer

crosses the bar to take up station
beside us. He declares he's glad
we're here, glad we fetched them back
alive, says 'twas different in the auld times.

In the auld times, he says, 'twas different –
on nights such as this they dragged
a grapnel along the grey water's bed,
and often as not snagged the afterworld.

Along the grey water's bed their grapnel
rent unanswered prayers, unused flares,
a mother's dream as they hooked her child
and brought him, punctured, to the surface.

Watermarked

i.m Seamus Heaney

At thirteen, my chosen poem *Rite of Spring*, though disallowed
in lessons, revealed the thrill of ambiguity in its suggestion
of the carnal; a stark rite of passage. Today, I'll stow your verse in
   the bow
of my craft, guard your *Door into the Dark*, a treasured first
   impression.
I'll row rhyme to the centre of October, then further into open
   water
to catch a zephyr, to drift the lake's cool-blue afternoon.
Here, a scribbled sky's unstrung pearl slips through its border,
and, watermarked, mimics moon. There, a skein of geese assumes
the rusty air of the potting-shed door, their rising path oblique.
But, being no longer here nor there I must find you
now in *Opened Ground*, take up your *Postscript* and speak
your words to Clare's wild shore where, due
west on Slieve Aughty, a stony up-againstness is halting
time at Bohatch Dolmen, where they appear, *all standing
   waiting*.

Light Air

Half past midnight, and I had gone to bed with *Sense and
   Sensibility.*
Just as Willoughby was to sweep Marianne into his arms,
my pager sounded. Wind hurled itself repeatedly and without
   civility,
against the house. It harried the gloom without alarm,
and, through the leaky window frames, howled in mad delight
once it caught itself hiding in the woods. In modest nightgown –
(thirty yards of Georgian cotton) – and husband's gum boots,
   (O no troglodyte
am I), I took myself to Station, then quickly moved when
   frowns
from fellow crew outlined how nightgown, 'gainst a stout
   searchlight, reveals.
Launched inside the ten with neither moon nor stars to guide us,
we unsealed the dark with a many-thousand candelabra flung
   squealing
past the wind. With night's black-feathered cloak unfurled, thus
we found them deep inside Coose Bay, all well and full of
   gladness.
Then with toe and heel we set a dance for home, subtle in our
   deftness.

The Shout

The wind is inconsolable.

Crouching to vent my drysuit,
I hear gravel scatter, greeting calls
as my fellow crew rush to change
for the Shout. What's out there?

they ask. I tell them what I know.
It's seven and gusting, our Launching
Authority says. *It'll be rough by Parker's.*
This we already know.

One, two whacks on my back tell me
crew are seated, feet in stirrups.
With an all-clear port and starboard,
I open the throttle, launch into the maelstrom.

The water is bruised purple and black.
Our ballast tank full equals the weight
of three men in the bow, keeps our
nose down as we face the turmoil

of this inland sea. On our port side,
a conspiracy of cormorants
huddle on Salmon Island's
rocky crop, keeping watch.

In open water the waves
heap up, retching, dumping turf-
stained lake across our bow. I power
up the face then throttle off

so we don't take flight at the crest,
pendulum to a bow-over-
stern capsize. By Hare Island
a turn to port and a beam sea

makes us wary of rogue waves
quarter side on. I hold a reserve
on the helm – to power us away
from harm if needed, and, for safety,

steer in at forty-five degrees.
At Parker's Point with a boxing sea
and pyramid waves, we read all
movement, call it as I steer behind,

in front and away from breakers.
In my earpiece our Radio
Operator, seated behind me, transmits
our location every fifteen, to Valentia.

We see them ahead below the Middle
Ground, side on to weather and sliding
down the shoulder of a breaking wave.
But with nothing beneath them,

their anchor drags before their makeshift
drogue snaps them to, bow to weather.
I ease us in from windward.
A crew climbs across, carrying

a radio, a smile, First Aid.
Eight on board, all below
except the skipper, luminescent
in his orange lifejacket.

My crew shouts to those below,
reassures them. After a quick survey
of frightened faces he gets to,
sets up a bridle before he

and the skipper haul in anchor
and drogue. I helm into wind to
cross the T and pass the tow, count
sets as crew pays out line until I call,

secure the tow. Making way,
we radio back 'centre your rudder'.
With an eye to the swell, the wind
and boat astern, we plough a trough,

ease back as the line groans, then into weather
we point west through Scarriff Bay, steering clear
of the Middle Ground. In the lee of Bushy Island,
we shorten the tow, safe harbour in sight at last.

To Touch the Sky

A reach
to the Mountaineer,
we gybe round,
stay upright,
despite the squall squaring
up from the Hare.

Running before
the wind, the boat
ahead broaches,
recovers,
death rolls by the lee,
and, over-canvased, upturns.

Rescue roars
past. The wind
is perdition's bellows
just howlin' for hell.
Clouds blacken for a God-
waked Sky as we sail to survive.

Detonations
behind us, our crew
says, are two
masts snapped, two
more over with a gust.
Sue and I struggle to

synchronise
helm and sheet. Our crew
cries, *I'm afraid,*
I can't do this …

She climbs the gunwale and leaps.
We lurch to windward,

and are mercilessly
pushed over. Submerged
I continue
to descend, down to the still
quiet beneath the lake's lid.
Tired … I try to kick,

to loosen
myself from the water's
drag. I will
not drown, not today –
my jacket obliges
me to surface.

I reach up,
attempt to touch the sky,
altered to
my underwater eyes.
My fingers break through,
are grasped and held fast.

Unknown in This House

So, how long must I wait?
You don't settle indoors do you?
Look around, all of this in your
honour, done just so for you:
Gilt, gold, tabernacle and cross.

And yet. This is sanctuary on those
quiet days, when nothing
enters but the silent hushings
of spirits in pews – as eager
and as equally disappointed

as the living, all stained by your
light, in palaces built from despair,
by men obsessed by symbols:
gilt, gold, tabernacle and sin.
The place of my kin where I am

welcomed but reminded it is not
my house, separated as we are
by denomination, wedded as we
are by our faith in the possibility
of good and the certainty of evil.

No, you are not here. I will stop
this now. You are not to be found
in a house where you are unknown.
In the unholy outdoors, navigating
the Latitudes of Whimsy,

I will oar my boat to the edge of your realm,
where you can catch me, not waiting for you.

Found Poem

*Ross Antarctic Expedition (1839–1843). J.D. Hooker's journal notes
on seeing Mount Erebus for the first time*

Captain Ross predicted the magnetic south lay
one hundred and sixty miles inland of us, nonetheless,
east to west a three-hundred-mile ice reef barred our way.

By April 1841 we had breached the 79th parallel
south, and there surveyed Antarctic lands
hitherto unknown, including this volcanic island where

"the water and the sky were both as blue,
or rather more intensely blue than I have seen
them in the tropics, and all the coast one mass
of dazzlingly beautiful peaks of snow, which,
when the sun approaches the horizon, reflected

the most brilliant tints of golden, yellow and scarlet.
And then to see the dark cloud, tinged with flame,
rising from the volcano in a perfect unbroken column;
one side jet black, the other giving back the colours
of the sun, sometimes turning off at a right angle

by some current of wind, and stretching many miles
to leeward. A sight surpassing every thing that can be
imagined, heightened by the consciousness that we
have penetrated under the guidance of our Commander,
into regions far beyond what was ever deemed practicable,

caused a feeling of awe to steal over us, at the consideration
of our comparative insignificance and helplessness,
and at the same time an indescribable feeling
of the greatness of the Creator in the works of his hand."

We named the mountain Erebus, God of Darkness, son of Chaos, and mapped co-ordinates of the island we named, Ross Island, that future expeditions to these ice-bound seas, might journey inland.

II

We who are dead
Depend on the imagination
Facts are useless to us.
They are always the facts of life.

from *The Colour Blue* by Tom Disch

Conceive

*Let us imagine sleep suddenly like a child's shadow
leaping
round the corner.*
— *George Szirtes [Tweet March 21, 2014]*

They are shown
back-lit negatives.
Trembling there
a caged pump,
fugitive and rare. They're told
to hope for winter.

Latin name,
chordae tendineae.
Heart strings torn
from their winch,
fastened to a fleet, dropped fall,
that cannot winter.

No keepsakes.
None. They're wrought by the
negatives
but must cope –
he carves yew, while she unlearns
their child's winter cry.

The Sea

Full of the sea.
At spring tide
and gibbous moon
it splashes the rocky
outcrops of his skull,
spills out of caves
onto his face.
That is the sea
washing his face.

That sound,
like fingertips tapping
the skin of a drum,
is from him,
his pan-systolic murmur.
He is not broken,
though the cello
in his lungs would
play in minor key.

And why he treads water
here, is to know the tumble
of the breaking waves,
the better to swim
for shore with the following sea.

A Rite

I swaddle the child and place her
with her mother. *Eve*, she says
and rocks her softly, softly.

A cry gathers, wave-like, inside her,
and, when it is released, this woman,
sorrowing, is both raging sea
and capsized emptied vessel.

She is held off from the peril of herself
by her partner, who in his turn clings
to calm. But, losing his grip against
her spindrift, he too tastes sea salt.

The Chaplain can offer only a blessing;
Baptism is for the living, and not this
innocent who remains with original sin.
We invite him to leave. And then,

following a ceremonial bathing
of mother and child, we cleanse Eve,
by intention, and with water.

Thoughtless

The polar bear inside
her head brought the blizzard.
He galumphs around behind
her eyes, licks saltwater
from her lens, then mists them
over with his constant panting.
He feeds on grey matter –
grinds his teeth on every little thought,
gifts her memories to snowy silence.

When she asks her husband
what'll happen when she disappears
into the frozen hush of herself,
he holds her close, says, *we won't
notice the difference.* That used to be
their joke. The polar bear,
inside the emptying room
of her mind, sits down
with a thump.

Coma Berenices

He ventured to that other land, its star sign Cancer,
a land edged by a Callous Sea that took his sister.
He grew a constellation behind his eyes that answered
to night's Dark Rider, was irradiated by the sun's cold glister.
She would have given herself to have him well, to return that
constellation to the heavens. What else did she possess
to bargain with? For Ptolemy, Berenice gave her plaited
hair to Aphrodite and he came home. We see her success
in Coma Berenices' nocturnal diadem. Now neither infirm
nor to blame but oh so young (not yet twenty-two), she shears
her head. Not in protest, but as bequest to the gods, to affirm
her readiness to outrun him in that dreadful race, to dispel his
    fears.
And as other galaxies gathered in his sight, she knew his time
was modulated by worlds at war inside his mind; crumbling but
    sublime.

Escape Route

Dad set twelve ladders in the barren crusted earth. For his
children.
Our darkest ravens sky-locked each top rung.

Living

A sort of quantum
mischief that answers to its
own logic, even
and especially when no question
has been posed, we call
being, sentient, alive.

Life's blank delicacy
is a fine gauze dressing we
mark with our first breath,
tear through with our last.
Living is to be this side
of what we imprudently
imagine an impregnable blind.

We are but sea-bleached stones
warmed by the sun, held in each
other's palm, loose in
each other's heart, and
miming unanswered murmurations,
we startle the sky with our flight.

The House of Silence

Annamakerrig, November 2014

I knew a man whose watercolour
eyes leaked turf-stained rivers, rivers
that flowed nightly through his dreams,
left arid in his unable season.

I knew a man who drove posts
into the earth, to seal a patch of *hungry
grass*, *hungry grass* that drove through
soil with the ferocity of famine.

I knew a man who dug deep holes
in the cold, hard ground, hoping to
uncover the truth of himself, but
finding only what lies beneath.

I came to this place to be alone
with my words, to rearrange the code.
Three dead men sat in my car and came
with me to the house of silence.

Now I've described the song at their
heart's core, they've followed the wolf,
lame to the woods. They wish me luck,
tell me they'll return in a week.

Back

A map of the Namib Desert grew
on my back, its uttermost northerly
reaches extended scapula to scapula,
its most southerly tip rested over
my fifth lumbar vertebrae –
a desert continent on my skin.

And like the Namib, regions were dry
barren wastelands, blistered by sun
and longing for the cool respite of water.
And like the Namib, the landscape on
my back lay excoriated and unseen
under one hundred and eighty days of fog.

And you tell me this abrasion of my asylum
layer is my desert's *Sperrgebiet*, its prohibited
zone, that this indifferent breach is exacted
by my mind on my body as a mark of dread?
Dread of my father's dying. I resent this symptom
of betrayal, this signal of my silent panic.

The Thing We Carry Now

i

Even had I known that Tuesday
was the last we'd have to talk,
I wouldn't have changed a thing.

He asked me to recite the names
of my seven brothers, four sisters,
an old family game, then stumbled

when his turn came. He persisted
'till he'd named us steps on stairs,
and after I'd shared a thought,

he said, "I'd love you to meet my daughter
Nell, I think you'd get along." I'd like
to meet her too, I said, resisting

the urge to say, here I am, I'm here.
My share as Dad's nurse, *daughter*
in parenthesis 'till he came through.

Later, when I'd kissed his forehead,
said, "Until next Tuesday, Dad,"
he smiled and said, 'Love you, Nell."

The calls, early of course, only two days later, was it only two days later, my Mom says he's been unresponsive since 2 a.m., my brother says, *Come home, Nell,* my sister says, *Come home, Nell,* I'm already on my way, I talk to myself, I say things like, Dad's been here before, I think of the time, years ago, he caught me talking to myself and said *It's okay to talk to yourself, Nell, I do it all the time, it's answering back that spells trouble.* I could never spell, I know when I see him I'll know, and when I saw him I knew, *rage, rage against the dying of the light,* Mom is strong, Dad's beautiful white-haired girl, but we mind her, we are fierce in our minding of her, we fly home, his flock returning, our parent's room our ward, Peter calls, he listens, I talk-cry, the hospice nurse brings the comfort things, we do the rest, nursing our father, all of us with Mom, in the room with Dad, then He arrives, dressed as Granddad, I'd seen him before, weeks before, different guise, but he'd left when Dad sat up, He sits with us now, long bony knees crossed, I know this time he's here to stay, dressed as my Granddad so to give death a familiar face, *and especially when red angels lit from his pipe and set his chest aglow with rubies, did I love my Granddad, in the holiest clothes in all the land,* He moves among us, unlit pipe between his teeth, waiting, giving us time to get used to this, we will never get used to this, none of us say, death is in the room with us, it would be superfluous, I talk loudly into Dad's ear, explaining, my sister says, *Nell, Dad's dying, not deaf,* and because this is something Dad might say, we smile and talk takes on an everyday pitch, we pass round family photographs, travel back in time, our families make us go eat, sleep, we are not hungry, but we eat, we sleep, fitfully, we gather again, we say the same prayer now, *go gentle …* four days, more nights, vigil, the loneliest word in the room, and finally, whatever might be called *lightfall* comes among us, connecting us to Dad and to each other, in this terrible privilege.

iii

It is the thing we carry now,
the weight of cold clay.
And here, a stopped clock,
a torn sail, a brass scales,
a box of useless broken measures
that cannot balance
empty chair with hollow gestures.

It is the thing we carry now.

A presence,
they said I'd sense you,
a presence
standing by.
I called out your name. DAD!
Hush-hush. Liars all.

An absence,
absolute absence.
You're gone, Dad
and that's it.
I called out your name. DAD!
Silence *charged* at me.

Where are you?
I want to show you
the barn owl
in our woods,
wraithlike, a stitched-to-sky bird,
who-too prefers dead

white silence.
Become an owl, Dad.
You wouldn't
have to talk.
Be that nocturnal creature,
white silence in flight.

New Year's Eve / Old Year's Day

We are the survivors
who wait by the barricade
for the slow countdown.
Some of our dead slip through,
stand beside us, unsteady, unclothed, low –
we cannot take them with us.

The cry goes up for cheer,
smile, they demand, *be merry*.
Fireworks tear the stars
from the moon, pock the night
with dissimulated Armageddon,
the awed throng pitches forward.

If not in groups then kinfolk
keep in hailing distance,
their calls, inmost, distinctive,
provisional. My Dad sees me first.
He's changed; parchment against bone,
eyes gone the colour of vertigo.

I am a smashed pane
that lets the rained downpour in,
in to vacant tenure.
As the countdown begins
there's a clamour for the barricade,
and this is where we're obliged to live on.

Sage

She lived with us for three days after she drowned.

The old fishermen tied their boats along the quay and joined the gathering crowd on the Cobb. They stood with their backs to the weather, against the spindrift carried inland on artic winds. One removed his cap, said, *the sea has that wee bairn now*. I didn't dare speak, say, *no, she's here, beside me*.

I was nine. It was the year Winter wouldn't let go, opening her mouth at the sea's sharp edge, to belch black sticking clouds over the sun. Cold rain lashed down like a punishment on our country, washing away everything that mattered.

She came into my dreams one squally Saturday night, and, by morning, had struggled down to my world, ready to stay. I was glad of a new friend who was ready to stay.

Granddad knew she was there. He caught odd glimpses when she darkened near candlelight. He knew too well the mouldy brown smell people had, when they came out of the sea, fusty, he called it. She gave off that smell every so often. I suspected Granddad worried about her, but he was never afraid.

She was nine too. Still, we were both a little shy of each other. She had freckles in her green eyes, and her top teeth were crooked. I spoke to her in my glad voice; I never wanted her to see I was sad for her. Granddad said *pity is a terrible cruelty altogether*. I didn't pity her, even if she didn't know she was dead but not yet gone.

When she followed me to school, I very nearly said, if I were drowned and dead but not yet gone, I wouldn't go to school.

She cried just the once. It was when Teacher caned me for talking to no one at playtime. Teacher said only bad children had *imaginary friends*. She caned me again when I pointed out the long shadows, huddled round her desk. My friend had tiny flecks in her tears, which I decided were fishes. I told her she must be part mermaid. That made her smile.

She asked if she could stay, but Granddad said she needed to *stay going*. He burnt sage and walked through the house, gathering her up. We followed him, laughing as we played hopscotch in his shadows. I held her cold hand, but I could never warm her up.

They were collecting by the North Point woods, waiting for her. Granddad asked how many. I told him there were more than I'd ever known before. He said, *you don't say, a lost child arouses compassion even amongst the dead.*

She went, not looking back, not once.

Later, when I asked if any creatures swam in my tears, Granddad looked closely at my eyes, smiled, and said, *No, not even one.*

Leave-taking

And as I wave them off,
Quiet comes to stand
beside me. She smiles too
at the inexpert weave
of the car backing up the yard.
The cheerful toot-toot on the
horn as they drive under the
arch and back to the world
reminds me that all that occupies
the space between me
and loneliness is quiet.

CPSIA information can be obtained
at www.ICGtesting.com
Printed in the USA
BVOW06s1039020117
472342BV00001B/157/P